Contents

The Ramblers' Association promotes country walking and protects rights of way. Having successfully campaigned in recent years for access to open country and Forestry Commission woodland, we now have our sights set on securing public access to remaining stretches of the coast of England and Wales. The RA plays a major role in securing legislation to protect our paths and countryside. Please give your support by becoming a member.
Write to: The Ramblers' Association, Camelford House, 87-90 Albert Embankment, London SE1 7TW Tel: 020 73398500 Website: www.ramblers.org.uk

Berkshire Area
The RA has seven Groups across the County. Each Group arranges its own programme of walks and endeavours to monitor local footpaths, to seek improvements and oppose any threats to them. For details contact:
Mr John Moules, 50 Qualitas, Roman Hill, Bracknell, Berkshire RG12 7QG.

Broadmoor Lane and Sonning Village

This short walk features the unspoilt historic village of Sonning-on-Thames, passes through the fields of Sonning Farm, and returns along a peaceful stretch of the riverside above St Patrick's Stream. A circular walk in Sonning has only been possible since the University of Reading agreed in 1991 to the creation of a permitted path across their land at Sonning Farm.

Distance: 3 miles
OS Map: Explorer 159 Reading
Start: From Sonning Lane (B4446) where it reaches the old part of the village. Grid ref: 756 754

With your back to the impressive gateway of Bishop's Close (North Lodge) join the footway in front of Turpins (Dick's aunt lived here). Stretching ahead on either side (Pearson Road) is surely the quintessential architecture of an English village. The art and craftsmanship of more than five centuries are here; timber-framed cottages, elegant Georgian façades and handsome Victorian brickwork, all in complete harmony without the help of any 'planners'!

1 Just before the end of Pearson Rd, cross Pound Lane and at roundabout bear right up Charvil Lane. Where footway on right ends, carefully cross the road, opposite the entrance to Sonning Farm to pass through kissing gate. This was jointly funded by East Berks Ramblers and Sonning Parish Council. It marks the start of what is shown on old maps as Broadmoor Lane. It is now a permitted path, following a suggestion made by the Ramblers.

Follow the farm track ahead, concrete at first, then gravel, slowly descending with open views. On reaching farm buildings on right, go straight on along grassy track, to leave the fields by wooden swing-gate. Turn left along tarmac lane (Milestone Avenue) soon to reach metal road bridge over St Patrick's Stream.

2 A right of way continues ahead here towards Wargrave, but our route turns left immediately before the bridge, shortly joining the riverside. The path on the opposite bank, designated in 1996 as the Thames Path National Trail, makes this one of the all too rare stretches where one can walk for any distance on both sides of the river. So now stroll, or otherwise as the mood takes you, for a mile along this seemingly remote part of the river to reach the best-known view of Sonning, the old red-brick bridge, which today shoulders loads never dreamt of by its 18th-century

builders. Can you spot all eleven arches?

3 To continue the walk, pass under the bridge and follow the riverside, known here as Thames Parade. Before turning left, on reaching the iron railings of Holme Park (Reading Blue Coat School), you may like to visit the lock just upstream, first opened in 1773. The gravel path leads away from the river to the parish church of St Andrew. The many young trees in the churchyard were planted to restore the storm damage of January 1990. Go straight across the churchyard to leave by swing-gate in front of the Bull Inn and follow the roadway ahead.

The Bull was once a pilgrims' hostelry and has always belonged to the church. The wall on the left conceals the Deanery Garden, a house built in 1901 by Edward Lutyens with gardens designed by Gertrude Jekyll. The site was once part of a palace held by the Bishops of Salisbury, hence the name. At road junction look left to see an antique pump, given to the village in 1846 by Robert Palmer, 'squire' of Sonning for fifty years.

Now turn right, up High Street and at the top right again to return to start.

The riverside path

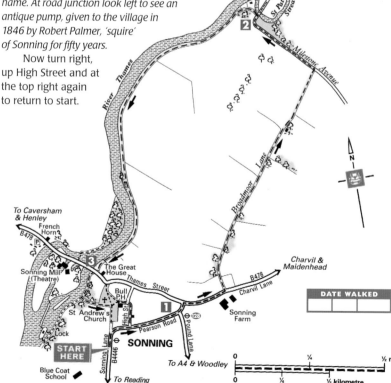

Binfield Heath and Shiplake Woods

This circular walk is through the peaceful, pleasant farmland and woodland to the west of Shiplake. Within the route is described a shorter alternative.

Distance: 3¼ or 4 miles
OS Map: Explorer 159 Reading
Start: Recreation Ground (limited road-side parking) at Binfield Heath. Grid ref: 746 786

With your back to entrance to Recreation Ground, turn right along road and just before Post Office stores fork left along unmade road, Heathfield Avenue. Just after first pair of red-brick cottages on left, fork left into narrow fenced and hedged path between gardens. Cross gravel road and continue straight on, shortly to enter field at stile. Go half-right through middle of field to join and follow hedge on right. Pass into next field at gap in hedge and at bottom of descent enter woodland strip beside stile ahead. After

further stile at top of climb, keep straight on across middle of field to stile into High Wood. Here continue ahead on way-marked (painted white arrows) woodland path.

1 Emerging from woodland, keep straight on along drive, tarmac at first, with paddock fence on right. At kink in drive, pass Upper Bolney House on right and continue on concrete track. Where roadway bends left, by Little Spinneys, turn sharp right through gateway and head across middle of field to reach right-hand end of woodland ahead − Shiplake Woods.

Continue ahead along footpath and on emerging from woods follow broad grassy track. Look left along here for distant views of Bowsey Hill on far side of Thames Valley. At junction with broad gravel track, turn right along it for about 200 yards toward property on right. Here turn left down edge of field, with hedge on right, to road ahead and choice of route.

2 For the shorter route turn right along the road past the White Hart for

Keeping to the definitive path – near Shiplake Copse

about 100 yards, then turn right up steps to follow path along top of bank parallel with road below. Rejoin road shortly before field entrance, and follow it for about 300 yards. Opposite end of tall flint wall, turn right along field-edge path beside Teapot Cottage. At field corner turn half-left in next field towards right of large tree. Here pass in front of two bungalows and continue on gravel roadway to return to start.

To continue the longer walk, cross road and pass through the stile-way into field ahead, follow the cross-field path behind the White Hart, towards double power-line poles on left of copse. On reaching copse, bear right to next power-line pole and here turn half-right again, up through middle of field. Cross a grass track, keeping straight on with field boundary nearby on right, at first, then downhill to enter Shiplake Copse ahead, at corner of field.

3 Now bear right along gently climbing woodland path. Finally leaving the trees, continue along headland of two fields with hedge on left. At road turn right, until at 'S' bend ahead, at beginning of village after Kings Common Close, turn left by metal barrier into Recreation Ground at start.

DATE WALKED

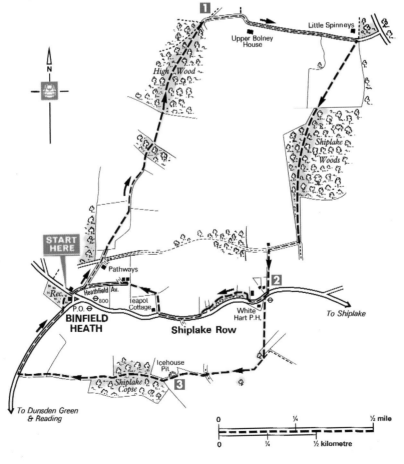

Morgan's Wood and Crowsley Park

This short circular walk to the east of Sonning Common is through some very pleasant Chiltern countryside and attractive parkland.

Distance: 3 miles

OS Map: Explorer 171 Chiltern Hills West

Start: Limited verge parking (Grid ref: 719 790) about ¼ mile along lane towards Dunsden Green from Bird in Hand on B481 (do not obstruct field entrance).

Facing Dunsden Green direction, continue along lane for about 200 yards to gap in hedgerow at signpost on left, just before two cottages at bend ahead. Turn left through middle of field (passing under power lines) to centre of woodland ahead – Morgan's Wood.

Enter wood at gap and follow waymarked path (painted white arrows) to soon have open field on right. At end of woodland, path continues, now fenced, beside field, then widens into grass track to The Well House on right. Shortly, at thatched Frieze Cottage, turn right along narrow lane for just over ¼ mile.

1 At T-junction turn left along road for some 150 yards, then turn right through side gate, past lodge on right, into Crowsley Park. The parkland is owned by the BBC (based at nearby Caversham Park) and is used as a satellite and terrestrial receiving station.

Keep along tarmac drive and when level with front of mansion, bear right through metal gate, as the right of way crosses corner of the enclosed grounds. *Much neglected in post war years, this splendid old house has been carefully restored since reverting recently to private ownership. Although its origins are something of a mystery, the exterior is 18th-century, the date 1734 appearing on the south front. Between 1844 and its acquisition by the BBC during the war, the*

The recently renovated Crowsley Park House

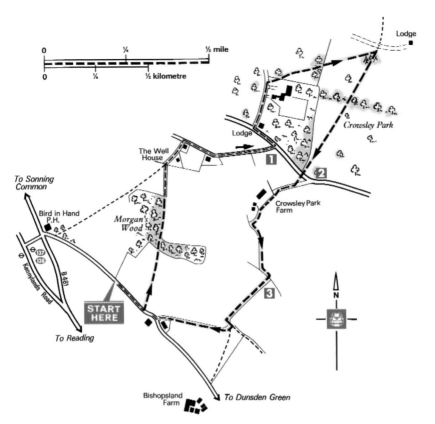

property was owned by the Baskerville family. Their coat of arms and crest can be seen high over the front porch.

A second metal gate leads into parkland beside the house. Here the path bears away from the railing fence to a stileway just beyond small group of mature trees. From the stileway go straight on across open parkland for about 250 yards towards a single large fir tree. A few yards beyond the tree *turn back sharp right* on path defined by wooden waymark posts. This soon crosses avenue of oaks (leading to house on right), then draws closer to fence and trees, finally to leave parkland at swing-gate in far corner.

2 Descend brick steps, cross road to stile opposite, and then cross corner of field to another stile, to turn right along metal drive leading to Crowsley Park Farm. Just before gates, bear left over stile and follow right-hand edge of large field. Path follows fence round corner of field and soon drops steeply downhill. Disregard wide field opening on right and almost at top of slope ahead, cross two stiles in hedgerow on right.

3 Now follow wide grass track ahead with hedge on left and where this meets junction of paths, turn sharp right, now with hedge on right. At end of field join track passing red-brick cottages and turn right along road to return to start.

DATE WALKED		

Peppard Common and Kidmore End

This circular walk is through gently undulating typical Chiltern countryside and does a complete circuit of Sonning Common

Distance: 7½ miles
OS Map: Explorer 171 Chiltern Hills West
Start: At or near Bishops Wood Sports Centre car park
Grid ref: 698 807

From Sports Centre turn right along Horsepond Road for some 125 yards, then turn left into gravel track. Pass through gap next to gate and after a further 50 yards, path through kissing gate on right and go half-left through middle of two fields. At bottom of dip continue in same direction, now uphill through two fields, beside tall hedge on left, to road (Wyfold Lane) after gate.

Turn right along lane and at road junction cross over, following lane to right of the Unicorn, then between Clare House and Manor View on right, enter up steps narrow path between railings. Follow winding path between

Photo by Don Flower

Kidmore End village pond

cottages to emerge on edge of Peppard Common. Continue down broad woodland track bearing right. When track starts to curve tightly right look out for path on left. Take this and after passing between wooden posts turn left again and descend down through wood. At clearing in valley bottom, bear right then left up steep narrow path in trees (with main road nearby on right) to reach edge of open common. Here turn right and shortly cross main road, keeping straight on across common to enter and follow Church Lane, past Peppard Primary School.

1 Pass the flint-faced All Saints Church (largely rebuilt around 1875). Continue on gravel track and in front of cottage ahead, turn right for a few paces, then left at stile. Follow left side of first field, pass through woodland strip, then continue down right side of next field past a rustic seat with a fine view, before turning right into broad hedged track. At top of slope pass left of Blounts Farm and shortly, with care, turn left along road. Just before end of copse on left, turn right up bank and across field to reach stile at right-hand end of woodland and then beside two fields to road. Turn left past Pond Farm Cottage down this narrow lane and at junction turn right for about ¼ mile, then right again, to Frieze Farm. Follow lane round left-hand bend and then immediately before thatched Frieze Cottage, turn right along gravel drive.

2 At The Well House bear right on grass track, shortly to cross stile beside gate and head across middle of field to stile at right-hand end of woodland. Maintain same direction through next two fields to reach road after stile. Now turn right and carefully cross road (B481) by the Bird in Hand. Enter swing-gate and go half-right over Kennylands Field (open space) to road on far side. Enter path to right of Winter's Folly

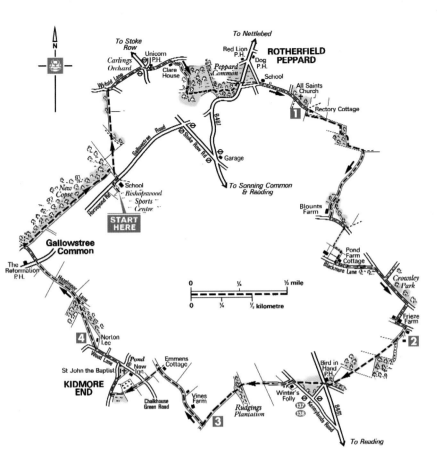

opposite and at end of short drive bear right, along broad grass path to left of triangular field. Cross stile in metal rails and go straight on through middle of field. Wide track then leads through trees and joins broad grass headland with fence on left.

3 After stile next to white farm gate turn right into tarmac drive. Passing left of Vines Farm continue on hedged track until, immediately after Emmens Cottage, turn left over stile and across field into narrow fenced path to road (Chalkhouse Green Rd) at Kidmore End. Cross over into Coopers Pightle, continue beside cemetery and then fence of play area. Turn right along road and walk through churchyard shortly ahead on right of the flint-faced St John the Baptist (consecrated in 1852). At road junction, by old well, it is

worth going right for some 50 yards to view the pretty village pond. To continue the walk go left past the well and along Wood Lane.

4 Just before bend in road, fork right by Norton Lee into fenced path. This continues through a beech wood to metal gate. Here bear left along tarmac road (Hazelmoor Lane). Reaching The Hamlet (Gallowstree Common) cross into road opposite and at bend, turn sharp right through stileway, then right again on bridleway, along edge of New Copse. Pass a cluster of houses and continue to far end of woods, before turning right along track to road, to return to start.

Withy Copse and Deadman's Lane

This mostly flat, circular walk explores the beautiful beech woods around Cane End, a hamlet situated 4 miles north-west of Reading.

Distance: 4½ miles
OS Map: Explorer 171 Chiltern Hills West
Start: From small lane (limited verge parking), east side of the Fox Inn, Cane End. Grid ref: 680 795

Facing main road (A4074) turn right on grass verge passing front of the Fox pub/restaurant and cross over the end of Horsepond Road. Immediately after white thatched Well Cottage ahead, turn right into tarmac drive. In about 50 yards, at entrance to property Clervaux, cross stile into field on left and follow hedge on right to stile at road (Park Lane), turning left along it.
1 Shortly ahead, turn right between a new property and an established bungalow. Go directly ahead passing stables on left to enter woods (Withy Copse) over stile. Just inside the woods bear left along woodland path, with conifer plantation on left at first.

Disregard crossing paths, and a permitted path off to the right, and follow the way-marked (painted white arrows) route ahead. On far side of copse, with fields in view ahead, path turns right to meet, at top of rise ahead, road opposite Kates Cottage. Here turn left along road, soon passing site (shown on OS map) of Castle Grove, a one-time fort.
2 At end of field on left, turn left onto track along edge of woodland with large field on left. Eventually reaching road ahead (Park Lane) beside a green barrier, turn right for a few yards along lane, then left along field-edge bridleway, with hedge on left. After passing solitary house on left, continue ahead on drive, becoming concrete, to road (A4074). Carefully cross over into road opposite (B4526) – Deadman's Lane.

Withy Copse beech woods

3 Keeping to verge on right, follow road for about ⅓ mile, then about 20 yards after 'SLOW' sign painted on road, turn left along edge of woods with birch plantation on left, followed by two fields. At end of second field, where other paths join, keep straight on, soon to have long thin field nearby on left. Follow path as it snakes between two small ponds and becomes hedged beside a cottage garden, leading into the tiny hamlet of Nuney Green.

4 Shortly, bear slightly right along gravel track until, immediately before a cottage on right, Crossways, turn left into woods on way-marked path. This becomes a wide stony track beside woods, now with field on right. At corner of field turn sharp right down sunken path, still with field on right. At

bottom corner of this field turn left and within 20 yards cross stile on left. Climb up through middle of field ahead to stile. Maintain same direction through woodland strip and across corner of field with three-storey Cane End House in view over the tall hedge to reach stile. Now bear right, pass through three bridle gates close together then diagonally through trees. After gate carefully cross road to return to start.

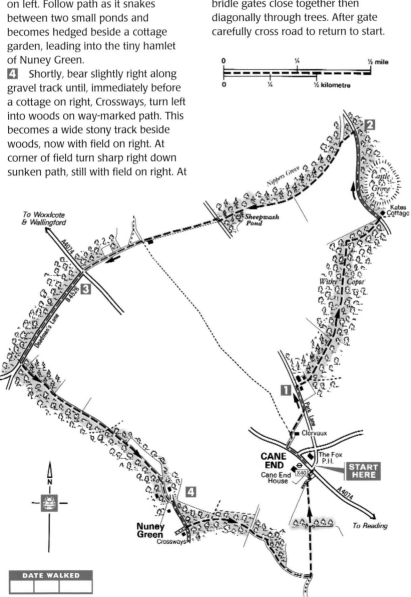

DATE WALKED

Whittles Farm and Collins End

This circular walk passes through the quiet beech woods around the hamlet of Nuney Green, descends steeply towards the historic Thames-side village of Mapledurham, then returns to Goring Heath through the beeches of Bottom Wood and across the open green of Collins End.

Distance: 4½ miles
OS Map: Explorer 159 Reading
Start: Former post office at Goring Heath cross roads. Grid ref: 657 792

With post office cottage on your right, cross into road ahead (Deadman's Lane) and after about 100 yards along road, fork right through metal gate into hedged track. After 120 yards cross stile into field on right. Follow field edge to left around property (Haw Farm) then take path straight ahead through second field to enter woods (Holme Copse) at stile. Disregard first crossing path and follow waymarked path ahead through woodland, to reach a path junction with corner of field nearby on left. Here cross stile, bear left and keep on through middle of further wood (Little College Wood) to reach stile on far side.

1 Follow field edge until fence bears right. Here our way goes straight on across the field to kissing gate beside entrance gates, turns right along road for about 200 yards, then again turns right over a stile, back into this same field (see map). Cross new driveway to Cane End House and after further stile continue ahead with trees then paddock fencing on left, to reach woodland. Just inside woods turn right along prominent track to emerge shortly at the tiny hamlet of Nuney Green. Here turn left along gravel track for about 45 yards, beside the bungalow Cross Ways, then fork right through pedestrian gate into hedged path.

Leaving property boundaries behind continue ahead on attractive woodland path. Shortly after field appears on left, leave woodland through metal kissing gate and go straight on between trees on left and fence on right to another gate at road. Cross over into tarmac drive leading up to Whittles Farm.

2 After farm buildings on right, continue on farm track until it turns left. Here turn right over stile and follow field edge beside trees and fence on left and fine views ahead over Mapledurham to the distant North Hampshire Downs. Go steeply downhill along the edge of two fields to reach valley bottom and turn left, past cottages and buildings of Bottom Farm. Follow farm drive to road and bear right along it, as far as a white painted house (once the village inn until closed by the Lord of the Manor in Victorian times).

3 At this point, to continue the walk, turn right into track − *or keep along the road if you wish to visit the picturesque Thames-side village of Mapledurham with its attractive flint and brick parish church of St Margaret. Mapledurham House and Mill (oldest surviving mill on the Thames) are open to the public during the summer (see footnote to Ramble 8).*

Now follow gently climbing fenced track for about ½ mile, then on approaching house in trees ahead (lodge to Hardwick House), turn right through kissing gate and bear left very steeply uphill to gate in top corner to enter Bottom Wood. Continue ahead on gently descending waymarked woodland path.

4 Keep straight on across shallow valley, climbing path in gulley beside rhododendrons to join tarmac track, after passing white cottage. Now follow this road past the scattered dwellings of Collins End and where road bends right, keep straight on into tree-lined path leading to road and start.

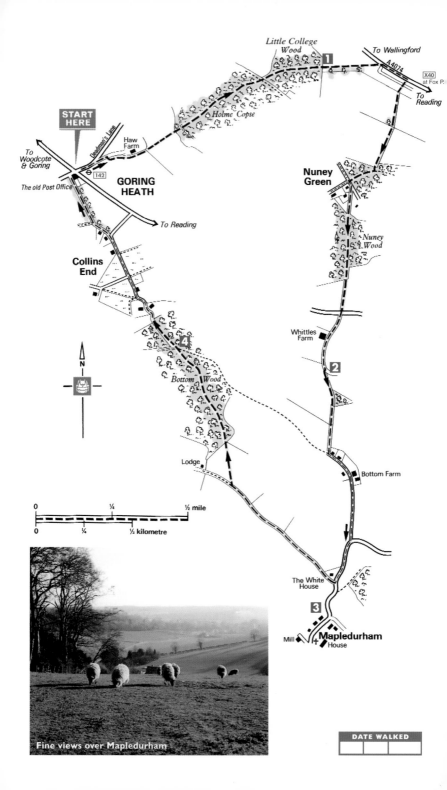

Little College Wood

To Wallingford

1

A4074

X40 at Fox P.

To Reading

Holme Copse

START HERE

Dysdman's Lane

Haw Farm

To Woodcote & Goring

142

GORING HEATH

The old Post Office

To Reading

Nuney Green

Nuney Wood

Collins End

Whittles Farm

2

4

Bottom Wood

N

Lodge

Bottom Farm

0   ¼   ½ mile

0   ¼   ½ kilometre

The White House

3

Mill

Mapledurham House

Fine views over Mapledurham

Westbury Farm and Sulham Woods

This circular walk through the rolling hills and flat meadows between Tilehurst and Pangbourne provides some magnificent views of the Chiltern Hills across the Thames Valley. The route also includes optional visits to the Thames and River Pang, but these will add about a mile to the walk.

Distance: 4½ miles
OS Map: Explorer 159 Reading
Start: Recreation Ground car park, Goosecroft Lane, Purley (off Beech Road). Grid ref: 652 760.

From car park entrance cross over Beech Road into gravel path opposite. Now turn right along road, until a few yards before roundabout, turn left down gravel roadway leading to bridge over railway. On far side turn left into fenced path beside railway cutting on left until at bridge ahead, turn right along tarmac road. At entrance to Westbury Farm turn left on roadway towards Springs Farm. After 'reception' on right, continue ahead on broad fenced drive, tarmac at first, then grass. Some 50 yards beyond end of fence on left, definitive path bears half left across field corner and continues along field edge with railway embankment on left. At end of field turn left to continue walk, or turn right along well-used path on near side of stream, to visit bank of the Thames opposite the historic Hardwick estate.

1 Go under railway on concrete road and shortly turn left along edge of field with stream on right. At main road (A329) ahead, with care cross over, turning right along footway. Immediately before filling station on left, turn left into tarmac path, Chiltern Walk, then after passing Nos. 10 to 7, turn right to pass in front of Nos. 6 to 1, to reach road ahead. Now turn right along road and shortly go left between Nos. 24 and 10 to reach two wooden swing gates. Here turn right, along side of meadow, for a short distance. At wooden footbridge in field either go straight on and through next field to visit banks of River Pang, or turn left over it and through middle of field.

... follow well-defined path towards tall trees ...

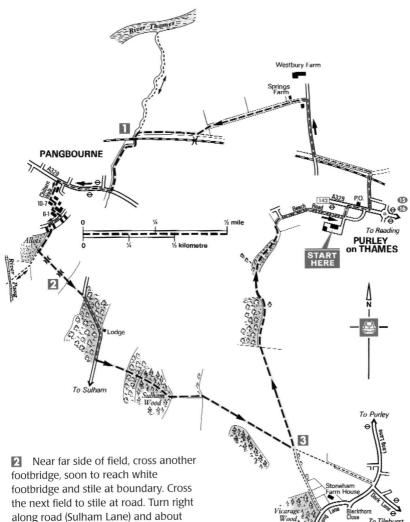

2 Near far side of field, cross another footbridge, soon to reach white footbridge and stile at boundary. Cross the next field to stile at road. Turn right along road (Sulham Lane) and about 150 yards after lodge on left, turn left over stile and up through middle of field to swing gate into Forestry Commission's Sulham Wood. Continue ahead up steps and straight on through the woodland to emerge on far side at Susie's Gate. At end of field fence on right, bear right into broad gravel track between open fields, to wooden post at path junction.

3 Here turn sharp left back on farm track towards distant woodland. Continue on, following path around outside edge of woodland. Then turn right on well-defined path (rising slightly) towards tall trees, then going straight on, following definitive path through middle of woodland strip. At far end, about halfway down side of field, turn right at kissing gate and shortly bear right along Beech Road to reach entrance of recreation ground on right at start.

DATE WALKED		

Newell's Lane and Chazey Wood

This circular walk is through pleasant rolling countryside between Caversham and Mapledurham. Within the route is described a shorter alternative.

Distance: 1½ or 4¾ miles
OS Map: Explorer 159 Reading
Start: Limited parking northern end of old road leading to the Pack Saddle pub, Chazey Heath. Grid ref: 695 772

From north end of the old road, with your back to the Pack Saddle, go ahead along footway on right of A4074, then about 20 yards after Rokeby Drive, with care turn left across road to stile and head mid-field towards woodland. On far side turn half-left along the field edge to reach road. Here turn left and at end of woodland (Curr's Copse) on right, turn right into sunken grassy track − Newell's Lane.

1 Where track reaches view of golf course ahead, follow it bearing right, then shortly left, to climb between banks. At top of slope bear left for about 100 yards and just beyond old gateway, at corner of woodland − here is the choice of routes.

For the shorter walk, bear slightly left beside wood (Noke End Shaw) then keep to hoggin-surfaced track turning left downhill across golf course, towards copse in valley. Follow the path up through middle of copse and on far side continue alongside new hedgerow on a grass path to reach hedged track (Jacksons Lane). Here turn left and rejoin the longer route.

For the longer walk bear right, follow the wide grassy track, with copse on left. Soon pass between the buildings of Rose Farm and continue on concrete farm drive. At junction, leave concrete road and keep straight on through field ahead towards middle of

The monument in Park Wood

woodland (Park Wood). Go through the woodland and on emerging from mature trees with open views ahead, ignore track in front but bear left downhill on narrow winding path. Since the devastating storm of 1987 the hillside has been completely replanted with oak, beech and ash.

2 After passing monument on left carefully follow steeply descending path to gate at bottom of hillside. Continue down middle of field, to meet concrete track at stile. Turn left here to continue the walk *or turn right to visit the picturesque Thames-side village of Mapledurham (no direct access to river) with its brick and flint parish church of St Margaret. Mapledurham House and Mill (the oldest surviving mill on the Thames) are open to the public at summer weekends.* *

To continue, follow the concrete road, passing Park Farm on left. Reaching a solitary bungalow, turn left up another concrete farm road, then at fork ahead go right (more concrete!) past farm buildings on right, towards Chazey Wood.

3 Follow winding road through the wood, eventually to reach junction of tracks (end of concrete!) with thatched cottage ahead. Here turn left along gravel bridleway (Jacksons Lane). At gap in hedge on left along here, the shorter walk rejoins.

4 Follow track to metal gate at the end, turn right along lane for about 100 yards and carefully cross main road (A4074) to return to the old road at start.

* Mapledurham House and Water Mill are open from Easter Sunday to end of September – Saturdays, Sundays and Public Holidays, 2pm – 5.30pm.

DATE WALKED

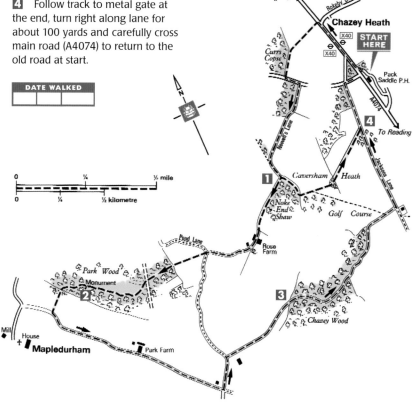

Tinker's Green and Hemdean Bottom

This circular walk, starting on the very outskirts of Reading, quickly leads into the peaceful farmland and woodland typical of the southern Chilterns.

Distance: 6 miles
OS Map: Explorer 159 Reading
Start: Car park at Mapledurham playing fields. Grid ref: 698 758

From entrance to Mapledurham playing fields, turn left along Upper Woodcote Road (A4074) for just over ¼ mile and between Nos. 185 and 187 turn left into gravel track. After stile ahead go half-right alongside fence on right, to stile in far corner. A few paces further on turn right along track (Jacksons Lane) to a nearby junction, then left for 100 yards along concrete drive. Now turn half-right onto path keeping young plantation on left. A flight of steps takes the path down into the valley, then climbs straight ahead to join track and reach trees (Noke End Shaw). Now turn right, with copse on left.

Local RA Group members near Tokers Green

1 At path junction, continue ahead on grassy track for about 100 yards to where this track (Newell's Lane) bends right. Here *keep straight on* into field passing three large trees on right, shortly to enter corner of field ahead. Go diagonally down middle of field to far corner, just left of white house. Now bear left along concrete track past Pithouse Farm to road ahead. Go straight over into narrow path across Trench Green and shortly keep straight on along road. Where road bends left, go straight ahead on bridleway through gateway past side of brick cottage on left and at far end of garden pass through metal gate. Some 40 yards ahead, turn right over stile and head through middle of long field to metal gate in far boundary, just to right of thatched Well Cottage at Tinker's Green.

2 Cross road (Sheepways Lane) into track and to pass buildings of Greendene Farm on left before road (A4074). Turn left along verge and after some 80 yards carefully cross road and stile under trees. Follow track through woodland keeping golf course nearby on right. Bear right and next to field gate enter narrower path. Follow path around two sides of clearing on left to Bardolph's Wood.

Follow the winding waymarked (painted white arrows) path. Where path divides taking the right fork avoids an awkward stile and unnecessary road walking. Now turn right along road for ¼ mile until, just after cul-de-sac, Skarries View, fork left and then turn sharp left, along tarmac road. At gateway to house ahead, fork right into gently descending track.

3 At bottom of hollow, cross stile ahead and climb steeply through middle of field to another stile where narrow hedged and fenced path leads to road. Here turn right along gravel track leading down and crossing road (Gravel Hill). Pass cottages to follow the open path ahead along Buggs Bottom.

4 At end of valley cross road between bollards and presently, at second lampost turn right. Pass between properties and go straight on up paved road (Tymawr). At top turn left up steps then right on tarmac path to emerge in Kidmore Road. Cross over, turning right, before turning left along Richmond Road. At far end turn right along Upper Woodcote Road (A4074) to return to playing fields on left at start.

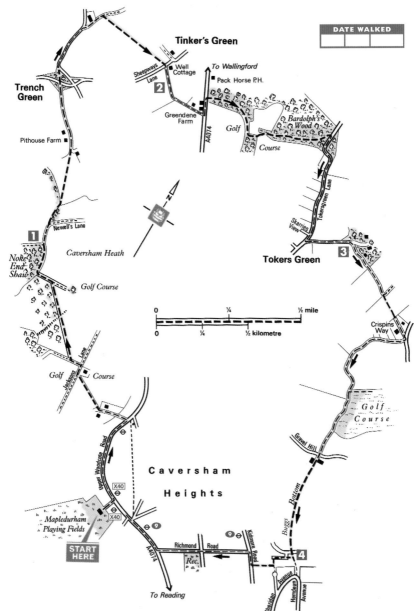

DATE WALKED

Balmore Walk and Sonning Eye

This circular walk, from the very heart of Reading, swiftly takes one into the Chiltern Hills and the Thames Valley to the north and east of the Borough.

Distance: about 10 miles
OS Map: Explorer 159 Reading
Start: Hills Meadow car park on B3345 by north side of Reading Bridge (free pm Sat/all day Sun). Grid ref: 719 741

From south end of car park, turn right on towpath under Reading Bridge and immediately fork right for about 70 yards, then bear right on grass beside tennis courts. Cross playing field ahead to join tarmac path. At road (Gosbrook Road) cross over and go diagonally left through small park, then turn right (Westfield Road) to traffic lights. Here cross over into Peppard Road opposite and immediately turn left up steps to reach and follow broad winding open green ridge – Balmore Walk.

1 After group of trees keep left down narrower gravel path to Rotherfield Way and turn left, then take second on right, Hemdean Road. At end of this road, at foot of Badgers Rise, go straight on, then along gravel track through Buggs Bottom. Cross lane (Gravel Hill) at Shipnell Cottages and go straight on up sunken tree-lined gulley. Near top of climb, immediately before stable buildings on right, turn right up bank over stile and along edge of golf course with fence on left. At wooden swing-gate in corner, turn left up hedged path. Shortly turn right (Tanners Lane) and at junction

turn right again, down road (Kidmore End Road). At end of golf course on right, turn left up Crawshay Drive. At top bend right, then very shortly turn left into Rosehill Park (curving to right) and at road junction ahead, turn left along Peppard Road (B481).

2 Immediately after Emmer Green Tower turn right into Tower Close, pass to left of No. 15 and at Marchwood

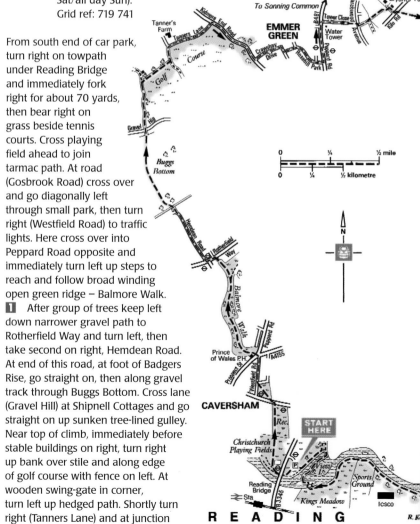

Avenue ahead, turn right for some 40 yards, then turn left into fenced path to right of No.12, leading to stile. Now follow hedge on right towards timber-clad buildings. Path ahead goes between low wall and hedge and along shingle drive from Bryants Farmhouse to road. Turn left along road for 25 yards to footpath on right and bear left through middle of field towards distant church.

3 At road turn right and follow bend passing All Saints church. At end of church wall on right use pedestrian gates to follow diagonal line through new parking area and across field. On far side turn right along lane, leading to Dunsden Green. Here bear right along road and about 60 yards beyond houses on left, turn left into field and follow right-hand side of facing hedge. At end of first field turn left into next one for about 150 yards to second tree in hedge. Now turn right and follow hedge, in direction of distant Sonning village.

4 At bottom of field turn left along a 'permitted path' (created to avoid the A4155 road below). Use steps down bank to cross road into lane beside the Flowing Spring. Some 60 yards beyond bridge, enter field on left by gate and follow edge of two fields with hedge and road on right. Continue alongside allotments and shortly, at road junction ahead, carefully cross over, pass through gate and along old road. At bend ahead, continue straight on to – Sonning Eye.

5 Follow lane through left-hand bend and in about 40 yards turn right along fenced tarmac path. Facing the French Horn, bear right along road and at far end of humped brick bridge, turn right and follow towpath for about 3 miles, crossing the 'horseshoe' bridge at Kennet Mouth. At Caversham Lock, turn right over upper lock gates. Follow path over weir and along side of View Island to reach eventually, on far bank, car park at start.

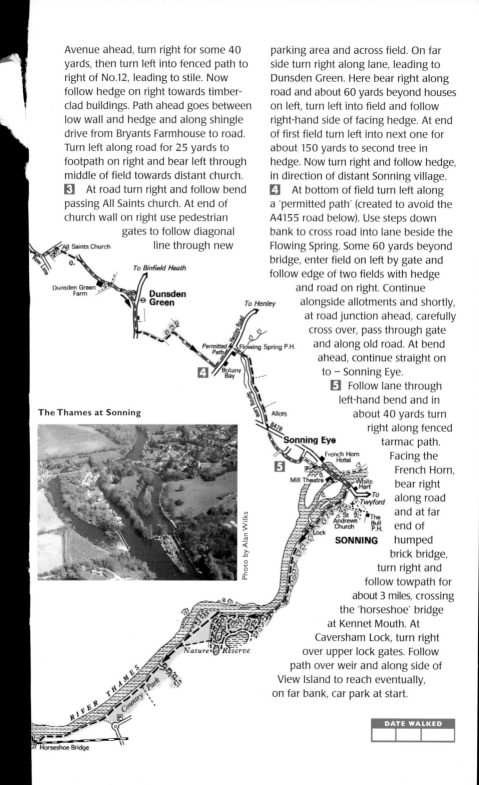

The Thames at Sonning

Photo by Alan Wilks

Nunhide Lane and Horsemoor Wood

This circular walk is through the beautiful rolling countryside immediately west of Reading, with extensive views over the hills surrounding the valley of the River Pang. Within the route is described a shorter alternative of 3¼ miles.

Distance: 3 ¼ or 5 miles
OS Map: Explorer 159 Reading
Start: Little Heath Road alongside Turnhams Farm recreation ground in Tilehurst. Grid ref: 654 728

John Wilder's folly

With your back to recreation ground, turn right along road and immediately after Turnhams House on right, turn right over stile into fenced path. Go straight on across next field to stile into woods (Harefield Copse). Descend woodland path, emerging to cross end of field using the new kissing gates. Continue straight on, down wide grass path through middle of very large field, passing, away on right, red-brick tower. *This is a folly built by the Rev. John Wilder, vicar of Sulham for 56 years until 1892, during which time he rebuilt the church and Sulham House, seen later on this walk.*

1 At bottom of field turn right along gravel farm road – Nunhide Lane. Pass buildings of Nunhide Farm on right and immediately after pair of red-brick cottages on left, fork left along side of large field with hedge on left. At end of field is your choice of route.

2 For the shorter walk of 3¼ miles, keep straight on along field edge with hedge and then Horsemoor Wood on left to the far end. Here turn right, in front of stile, to rejoin the longer route.

For the longer walk, turn left between new plantations towards the sound of the M4 motorway. After footbridge over stream, follow path through trees to cross M4 footbridge with spiral approaches.

Continue straight on with fence and large buildings (Malpas Farm) on right, then after passing beside metal gate by Pond Farm, follow tarmac road through double bend. Shortly, at next bend in road, just after overhead power cables, turn right along winding hedged track – a Restricted Byway. Eventually at point close to M4 turn left into fenced path with road on right. After zig-zag path, cross M4 on footway and then immediately turn right down flight of steps to stile at bottom. *(This is a permitted path, courtesy of Englefield Estate in 1999, steps built by the Ramblers).* Turn left in field, keep right of old hedge ahead, to reach stile by field entrance. *The hard surface here is the old road (pre M4) at Hogmoor Bridge over the River Pang.*

To Pangbourne

Moor Copse

River Pang

A340

Hogmoor Bridge

3

To Theale

3 Immediately before the bridge turn right along hedged gravel track until, at start of second field on left, turn left over stile next to metal gates and along left side of field with hedgerow trees close by. At next stile bear slightly right, mid-field, and after open gateway follow edge of field with hedgerow on left. Enter wood (Horsemoor Wood) ahead at stile and on emerging over footbridge, go on for some 50 yards to cross stile on right and rejoin shorter walk.

4 Now continue with fence on left. About half way along side of this field the path turns left and joins left-hand headland towards distant white building (Sulham House). Where field-edge bears left, head cross-field to exit at squeeze-stile in top corner (Nunhide Lane). To continue walk turn right *or turn left for some 80 yards to visit the impressive church of St Nicholas, Sulham. Built in 1832, it replaces one that had stood hereabouts since the late 13th-century. A plaque in the church tells us that the tower was restored after removal of a spire in 1959.*

5 Turning right up Nunhide Lane into Sulham Estate, follow this hedged track, then where it bends left, turn left through old metal swing-gate and head along well-defined grass path on slight ridge, to reach woods on far boundary. Within a few yards path turns left through trees, dipping in and out of nearby field, before climbing increasingly steeply to top corner of woods. Go straight on (Kiln Lane) with field on right, to road ahead. Here cross over, turning right along footway of Little Heath Road for about ½ mile to return to start beside recreation ground.

DATE WALKED
7 4 13

River Kennet and Sulhamstead Bannister

This circular walk, to the south of Theale, provides a marked contrast in scenery, from the waterways and lakes of the Lower Kennet Water Park to the undulating farmland and meadows around Sulhamstead. After prolonged rainfall some sections, especially the water meadows, can be wet underfoot.

Distance: 6¾ miles

OS Map: Explorer 159 Reading

Start: Easy verge parking near south end of Wigmore Lane (cul-de-sac), Theale. Grid ref: 633 703

Continue to south end of Wigmore Lane, with care cross railway line by stiles and turn right along fenced gravel path. At first power line pole ahead turn left, then after passing through copse cross metal footbridge and turn right along the winding north bank of the River Kennet. On reaching footbridge and weir, turn left across bridge, now to follow bank of Kennet and Avon Canal. At Sulhamstead swing bridge ahead turn right over bridge, then turn left and follow towpath for just over ½ mile.

Immediately after concrete footbridge, turn sharp right along winding path through woodland strip, with lakes on left, leading to road.

1 Turn left along this tree-lined lane, passing Fisherman's Cottage. At road junction continue ahead, then immediately after house on left, turn left beside gate up tarmac road and near entrance to Highways Depot continue on track curving right, beside trees (Brick Kiln Copse). Reaching open field ahead, bear slightly left up middle of field (passing to right of pylon) to find stile in corner to right of large property (The Old Manor). After stile turn right into gated gravel drive, passing Thane Cottage.

2 At road ahead turn right for a distance until, at white Keepers Cottage on left, fork left up private tarmac drive. On reaching concrete surface (before Home Farm) fork left into climbing grass track. Enter field ahead and follow fence on right to squeeze-way beside gate then on to stile in far corner. Here bear half-right to a further stile into St Michael's burial ground at Upper End, Sulhamstead Bannister. All that now remains of the flint-faced

Passing lock No.100 on the Kennet and Avon Canal

St Michael's Church, built only in 1912, is the porch − left as a shelter for funeral mourners.

3 At road ahead turn right past the Old School and at bend in road keep straight on over stile, then immediately left into enclosed path between paddocks. At stile ahead turn right down road (Kingston Lane). At first gap between fields on right, fork right and at field gate ahead turn left into fenced path hedgerow trees. In bottom corner cross stile into next field on right and immediately turn left. Follow two sides of this field with fence on left and in second corner turn left over stile, descending steeply to road opposite Glen Lodge. Here go a few paces left to road junction (Bottom Lane) and turn right.

4 Immediately before white Hazel Cottage on left, turn left over stile and down edge of field shortly to cross long wooden footbridge − built by Reading Ramblers in 1977 (see plaque midway along handrail). Now go straight on through water meadow ahead, with ditch on left to reach metal field gate by Sulhamstead swing-bridge. Now cross bridge and turn left to retrace route used at beginning of walk, to return to start.

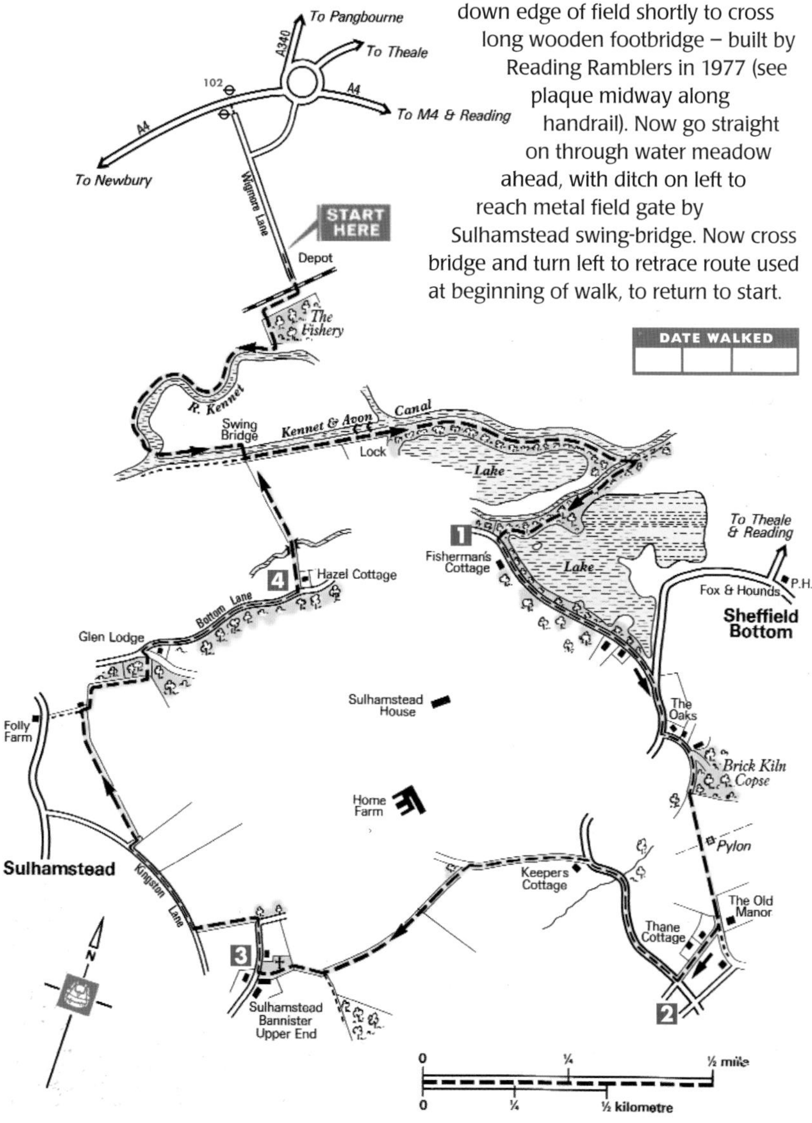

DATE WALKED		

To Pangbourne
To Theale
To M4 & Reading
To Newbury
A340
A4
102
Wigmore Lane

START HERE

Depot
The Fishery
R. Kennet
Swing Bridge
Kennet & Avon Canal
Lock
Lake
Lake
Fisherman's Cottage
1
Fox & Hounds
P.H.
Sheffield Bottom
To Theale & Reading
4 Hazel Cottage
Bottom Lane
Glen Lodge
Folly Farm
Sulhamstead House
Home Farm
The Oaks
Brick Kiln Copse
Pylon
Keepers Cottage
The Old Manor
Thane Cottage
Sulhamstead
Kingston Lane
3
Sulhamstead Bannister Upper End
2
N

0   ¼   ½ mile
0   ¼   ½ kilometre

Ufton Nervet and Shootersbrook Lane

This circular walk is through undulating farmland to the west of Burghfield, providing extensive views over and along the Kennet Valley.

Distance: 4 ½ miles
OS Map: Explorer 159 Reading
Start: South side of St Peter's Church, Ufton Nervet. Grid ref: 635 675

With the Church of St Peter (built in 1861) on your right, go ahead to road junction and turn left along Camp Road for about 50 yards. Here turn right along gravel track, soon fenced, leading to the interesting site of a medieval moat and fish ponds (see information board). Path continues ahead along side of field, then through gate leading past white-washed Ufton Court Lodge. Cross road, enter swing-gate ahead and straight along drive between broad avenue of oaks towards the Elizabethan front of Ufton Court. *The house dates from the late 15th-century, held by the Perkins family, Catholic recusants, who gave sanctuary to many priests in the days of Elizabeth I.*

1 At crossing track before house, turn right for 60 yards, then with an ancient oak ahead, fork left into a gravel track – Shootersbrook Lane. Follow this bridleway downhill (Brent's Gully), leading eventually up to Old Farm. In middle of yard turn right between large barns to enter broad track ahead. After some 75 yards turn half-right over stile. Go diagonally down middle of large field to stile at left-hand end of Noormoor Copse on right.

2 Here join track down edge of copse, cross stile by gate, then up slope of open field, beside mature trees. At crossing track, go straight on, now on grass path with Ashen Wood on right. After stile next to wooden gate, continue on fenced track to road by Middle Farm. Here turn left down

A local history lesson

road, keeping to verge on right.

3 On approaching road junction, fork right across grass to turn right up Church Lane, passing remains of chapel on left and Dog & Partridge (once a public house) on right. Immediately before Uftongreen Farm turn left through gateway and along track beside farm buildings and yard. Shortly on right, look to horizon for church spire at Ufton Nervet.

At end of field on left bear slightly right, alongside fence in next field. Pass through gap in hedge and on through next field with trees on left, leading to road by houses at Sulhamstead.

4 Now turn left along road and shortly, at junction, turn right with care up road (Kingston Lane). Near top of climb, turn left over stile into wide fenced strip. By first oak tree at top of rise, turn right over stile by metal gate and continue along road to Sulhamstead Bannister Upper End, passing the Old School and St Michael's burial ground on left, and Meales Farm

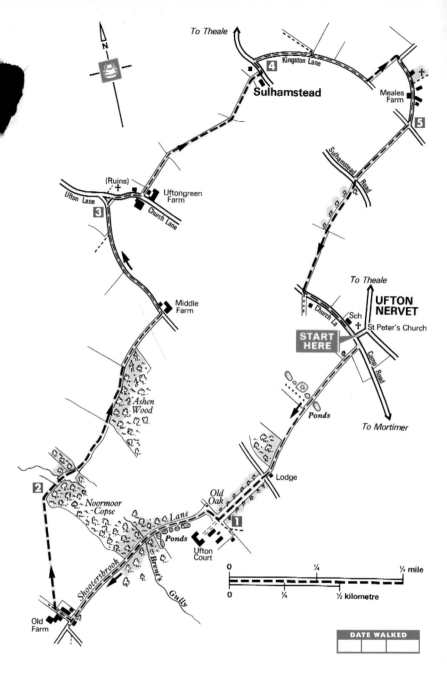

on right. All that remains of the flint-faced St Michael's Church, built only in 1912, is the porch, left as a shelter for funeral mourners.

5 At road junction cross over into fenced gravel track ahead. Cross next road ahead (Sulhamstead Road) and after stile in hedge, follow field-edge path ahead through two fields to reach road (Church Lane). Here turn left along lane to return to the church at start.

Pullen's Pond and Starvale Woods

This circular walk, north of Mortimer, has an attractive mixture of heathland, woodland and farmland, with some surprisingly pleasant open views to the east.

Distance: 4 miles

OS Map: Explorer 159 Reading

Start: Burghfield recreation ground car park (entry from Recreation Road). Grid ref: 651 668

From car park cross over Recreation Road into Fir's End road and at end take path half right diagonally through woodland to reach main road. Use pedestrian crossing to reach Bunces Lane opposite. A few yards round the bend in lane just ahead, turn left into narrow tarmac footpath. On joining gravel road (Spring Wood Lane) follow this through left-hand bend and at the end turn right down steps into, after small stream, woods ahead. At top of short climb fork left on well-defined bridleway until, on reaching gravel track, turn left along it. At red-brick cottage ahead follow track bearing right, shortly to pass on right at bottom of descent, Pullen's Pond.

1 Continue on climbing winding track to road (Goring Lane). Here turn left for some 40 yards, then sharp right along gravel track, shortly to turn left down another road (Lockram Lane). Just over 100 yards past Lockram Farmhouse on right, turn right through gap in fence. Pass to right of two mid-field trees before crossing wooden footbridge spanning Lockram Brook. Follow hedge up field ahead and look for gap in fence on left, where path passes tiny pond. Continue climbing this field to stile in top corner.

2 Here turn right along field-side track with fence on right. At end of first field, turn left downhill beside fence on right. At bottom corner of this field cross stile on right, to follow two sides of next large field, keeping fence and then trees on left. Just before buildings of Mann's Farm near top of climb, turn left through gap, down steps and over two footbridges to reach and turn right along road (Nightingale Lane).

The pond at Wokefield Common

Just after farm turn left through metal swing-gate and along right-hand side of field. Just before end of field turn right through swing-gate and bear right across middle of next field towards large oak tree in woodland ahead. Enter woodland and follow path, soon bearing right at fork, leading to road junction (Hammonds Heath).

3 Cross road and go straight on through swing gate along the edge of open space (the Fairground), parallel with road (Windmill Road) on right. On rejoining the road continue on footway until, just past Windmill Court, turn right into fenced footpath. Go straight on at fork and soon bear right through woodland (Windmill Common) to join a byway with field nearby on left. After crossing small valley with stream in bottom, pass to left of red-brick Bridges Farmhouse and turn right along road (Longmoor Lane). Where road bends right, turn left into broad path straight into woodland – Starvale Woods.

4 Follow footpath slowly curving left, then at path junction in slight hollow, turn right (bridleway) down between conifer plantations. Cross over Lockram Brook again and climb up to pass next to red-brick cottage (Starvale Cottage) on left. Cross drive and continue ahead over Wokefield Common to reach near side of pond. Here turn right along permitted path to soon reach road.

5 Cross road junction ahead and take main path (bridleway). Immediately after small pond on left, bear left. Cross gravel track and shortly pass over tiny stream into hedged surfaced path before houses ahead. Now turn left along gravel road (Palmers Lane), cross road ahead into fenced path and at the end, by Methodist church, turn right along road to return to car park at start.

BURGHFIELD COMMON

To Reading

Reading Road

Firs End

Recreation Ground

Hall

Burnes La.

P

START HERE

143 149

P.O.

Chapel

Spring Wood La.

To Padworth

Palmers Lane

Pullen's Pond

1

Lockram Lane

5

Pond

Goring Lane

Wokefield Common

Lockram Brook

Starvale Cottage

Starvale Woods

4

Longmoor Lane

Bridges Farm

Windmill Common

N

Hammonds Heath

Windmill Road

MORTIMER

The Fairground

3

0   ¼   ½ mile

0   ¼   ½ kilometre

2

Mann's Farm

Nightingale Lane

DATE WALKED

Admiral's Copse and Foudry Brook

This circular walk from Stratfield Mortimer is through the very pleasant and gently undulating rural landscape on the Berkshire/Hampshire border.

Distance: 4 ½ miles
OS Map: Explorer 159 Reading
Start: Mortimer Station

Leaving railway station by access road, turn left down road (Station Rd). Immediately after crossing bridge (Tun Bridge) over stream (Foudry Brook), turn right along road and beyond last house on left, turn left into a climbing footpath between fields. Cross road (Mortimer Lane) into field opposite by squeeze-stile and go straight ahead beside fence, becoming a wide grass strip with woodland on left. Now continue on to reach Wheat's Farm at top of climb.

1 Here pass between farm buildings, cross track and immediately turn left up bank. After some 60 yards cross stile ahead into narrow path. At path junction turn left over stile into field and after a few paces (by an oak) keep right along field edge with hedge on right. Pass small wooden gate on right and after a further 20 yards enter meadow ahead at stile. Go down the field to stile in bottom corner and continue along gravel track to road (The Street).

Arriving at Mortimer Station – 11 minutes from central Reading

Cross road and turn right along footway, then near top of rise turn left into Kiln Lane, soon descending as a gravel track. At bottom of descent, follow narrow path along wooden fence to left of Ashfield and cross footbridge over stream, soon to enter woodland – Admiral's Copse.

2 Follow well-defined path through length of woodland and then continue mid-field towards red-brick house at road (Drury Lane).

Here turn left and follow verge down to T-junction. Now turn right (Pitfield Lane) until immediately before bridge (Tanhouse Bridge) over Foudry Brook, turn left into short hedged path. After kissing gate, follow right side of meadow with stream nearby. In corner of field go straight on through a gate then over a stile, with stream between.

Shortly cross metal bridge over railway and head across field, open at first, later beside hedge and occasional oaks. At road turn left – the Berks/Hants county boundary and the Devil's Highway (the Roman road from Silchester to London).

3 Follow road to end of field on left then turn left next to old stile to follow field edge with hedge on right (which hides the remains of the quaintly named Ticklecorner Lane). Where hedge finishes bear right, now across an open field. Pass through wide gap in hedge into corner of field ahead and continue on grass path with hedge on left.

At end of this field, turn sharp left down hedged track leading into field. At end of hedge on right, bear right down middle of field and pass through rail tunnel. In next field, bear half-right towards concrete footbridge over Foudry Brook (yet again!) in far corner.

4 Do not cross bridge but turn right along the raised strip between field and stream, soon with fine view of the impressive stone church of St Mary, Stratfield Mortimer. Turn left

over stile and follow path over stream and along drive past Church Farmhouse to the road. Now turn right along footway, then right over Tun Bridge again, to return to station at start.

The distinctive spire of St Mary's, Stratfield Mortimer

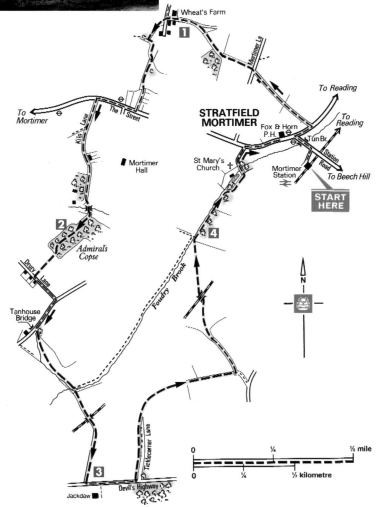

Lambwoodhill Common and Brook Farm

This circular walk from Grazeley is entirely on paths across farmland that have so far remained pleasantly untouched by the development taking place everywhere in Shinfield Parish on the opposite side of the A33 Swallowfield Bypass
    Walk while you may!

Distance: 3 ½ miles
OS Map: Explorer 159 Reading
Start: Church at Grazeley.
        Grid ref: 699 669

With your back to the small flint-faced Holy Trinity Church, turn right along the lane and where the tarmac ends shortly, continue ahead over stile beside metal gates into field-edge path keeping ditch on right. Look for tall way-mark post beside path and here bear half-left across the field (Lambwoodhill Common) in direction of distant pylon, to reach road (Pump Lane) through gap in hedge under trees near field corner.

1 Cross road into hedged track (Shepherdton Lane) opposite, pass under railway (Reading/Basingstoke line) and at end of lane turn left along another grass track with ditch and long field on left. For the next 1½ miles the route follows Shinfield parish boundary.

At end of field turn left over wide wooden bridleway bridge and along another hedged track, now with ditch on right. With care pass through swing gates either side of railway and continue ahead, becoming tarmac roadway, passing The Gables on left. With care cross road (Bloomfieldhatch Lane) ahead and after stile, keep along edge of large field with hedge on right, to reach road after ditch and stile.

2 Cross over, going slightly right, to enter through gateway a fenced drive leading to Brook Farm. Here continue ahead between house and stable buildings, then after gentle descent down tarmac drive, cross metal bridge (Reid's Bridge) over Foudry Brook. About 50 yards after bridge turn left into Woodcock Lane. Follow this hedged track with stream nearby on left until, at far end of trees on right, the path bears right up a slope and

Follow bridle path along Shinfield parish boundary

continues as a fenced track beside the Swallowfield bypass.

3 Cross minor road ahead, beside cattle grid, and continue along fenced bridleway, now with bank screening (thankfully) the bypass from view, eventually to pass through metal gate into field on left. With your back to this gate, go slightly right across middle of field to gateway onto wooden farm bridge over Foudry Brook. Now continue straight along field track with ditch on right to reach road ahead by school. Cross the road, pass round metal barrier and along left side of village hall field, to return to church and start.

A shared experience! ... RA members at the Emm Brook footbridge (Ramble 23)

DATE WALKED
18 03 12

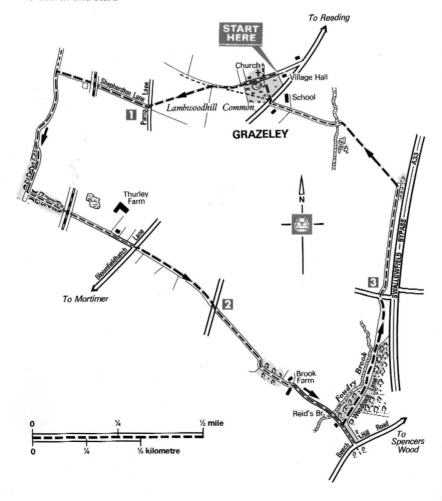

Woodcock Lane and Three Mile Cross

This mainly flat, circular walk immediately to the south of Reading is along the wooded paths and through the fields surrounding Spencers Wood

Distance: 3 ½ miles
OS Map: Explorer 159 Reading
Start: North end of cul-de-sac in the old A33 south of M4 junction 11.
Grid ref: 715 683

With your back to M4 motorway walk ahead along road. Opposite first facing house on left, Milestone Cottage (notice old milestone) take the path between the posts and at road ahead (Basingstoke Rd) with care cross over using traffic island. Pass through large metal gate into a byway signed 'Cart Track' – Woodcock Lane.

Follow this wide, well wooded byway for about ½ mile, keeping Swallowfield bypass nearby on right. At junction with metalled road beside old pond, maintain same direction using footway, for a short distance.

After passing Kingfisher Grove on left, continue ahead along the old lane for the next ¾ mile. We turn off some distance after bypass filling-station (seen through trees on right). Look for broad track turning left (Kiln Lane) and climb this tree-lined way with fields nearby on left. At top of rise pass two stiles on right (with pond between) and shortly bear left over stile and head across middle of field towards distant houses.

1 In far corner a stile leads onto Basingstoke Road. With care cross over, turning left along footway into the centre of Spencers Wood. *Originally Spencers Wood was one of the seven 'hundreds' of Windsor Forest; most of the development did not take place until the end of the 19th-century.*

Just after another milestone (exactly 1 mile south of the one where we started) turn right along Hyde End Road (B3349), then just past where road bends right, turn left along the length of Appletree Lane. At T-junction turn right (Clares Green Rd). At road junction, at end of field over hedge on

A parkland setting for this path in Spencers Wood

left, fork left and then turn left, to pass beside metal gate and follow drive ahead. Just before red-brick pavilion on edge of playing fields, bear left into hedged path and after about 75 yards, keep right into tree lined path parrallel to recreation ground.

2 After stile keep along edge of next two fields. Halfway along side of second field (with a view of Readings latest landmark directly ahead) cross stile into adjoining field and continue in same direction, now with hedgerow on left. After stile in field corner enter hedged path, shortly to reach road.

3 With care cross road turning right, then shortly at the small Wesleyan Chapel (Three Mile Cross Methodist Church of 1876) turn left into Grazeley Road. Just after first pair of houses on right, turn right along tarmac path. Enter path ahead through swing gate and follow hedged path to rejoin Woodcock Lane. Now turn right along this old byway and back over road ahead, to return to parking place at start.

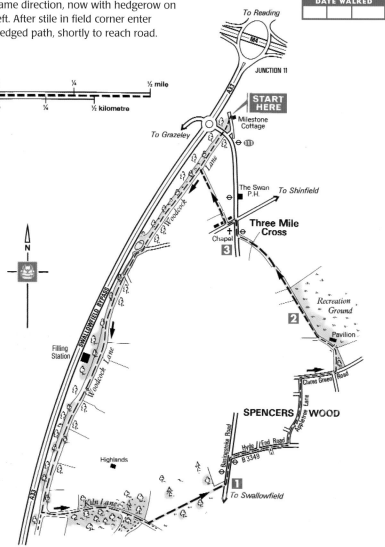

DATE WALKED

Shinfield Grange and Hall Farm

This circular walk to the west of Arborfield is over the rich farmland on both sides of the River Loddon. Fortunately proposals to build a bypass alongside the field-paths we use at the start of this walk were overturned recently at a public inquiry. Walk while you may!

Distance: 4 miles
OS Map: Explorer 159 Reading
Start: Closed end of Cutbush Lane, Shinfield. Ample roadside parking near Shinfield Grange (College of Estate Management).
Grid ref: 741 690

Facing Shinfield Grange, turn right and walk along Cutbush Lane for about 100 yards and turn left into tarmac drive. Just beyond end of evergreen hedge on right, turn right into hedged grass track. After stile beside metal gate ahead, bear right along side of long field with hedge on right. At end of field cross stile, then immediately turn sharp left through middle of field and over stiles

either side of short wooden footbridge. In next field follow diagonal line to stile in far corner, to enter narrow enclosed path beside property, once the Magpie & Parrot public house.

1 After stile-way ahead, turn left along verge of main Arborfield Road (A327), to bridge over River Loddon. Cross the road here and 70 yards beyond bridge, immediately before the half-timbered Bridge House, turn right into wide fenced path. At end of property on left cross stile and go diagonally across small field to a second stile then straight ahead through middle of field to pass a power-line pole. At end of this field cross an old road, known as Milkingbarn Lane. *This lane was once a public bridlepath; the Parish Council agreed in 1978 that it should be extinguished, in exchange for Pound Copse, passed through later in this walk.*

2 Continue ahead on broad grass track with hedge on left. At end of field on right, turn left over stile and follow edge of field with fence on right. At corner of field cross stile and turn left

A spring morning – just ¹⁄₂ mile south of the M4

along a permitted path through Pound Copse, with road nearby on right. At end of copse, rejoin public footpath coming from field on left. Pass through stile-way and turn left along road, Greensward Lane. At road junction ahead, turn right along main road (A327) for about 100 yards, then cross over into Church Lane and where this road bends right, turn left into a 'No Through Road'.

3 After right-hand bend, enter estate by white swing gate beside cattle grid. Continue ahead along tree-lined drive and immediately after crossing junction with concrete road, look left for remains of the earlier Arborfield Church. Continue ahead and shortly enter gravel track passing Hall Farm's Youngstock Unit. Continue on track to shortly re-cross the River Loddon and go straight on along fenced track. At end of field on right the track bears right, becoming hedged.

4 Where farm track bears right towards buildings of Oldhouse Farm go through swing gate and along hedged path. After 75 yards, turn right over stile into path, hedged and fenced at first. Where field opens out keep straight on to stile and footbridge at far side. Now follow fenced path beside two fields to stile at road, turning left to return to start.

DATE WALKED		

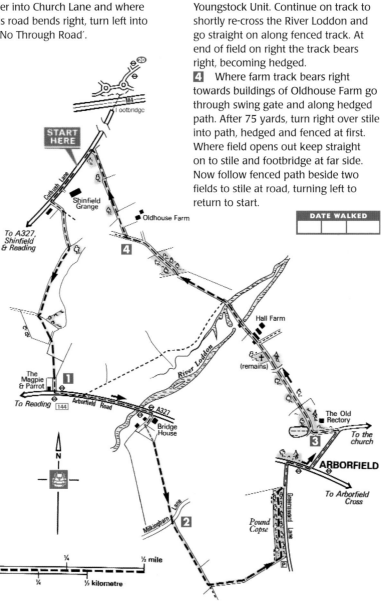

Carter's Hill and Barkham Brook

This circular walk includes the flat rich agricultural land and the gently undulating woodland to the north of Arborfield Cross. In winter and after wet weather some of the paths can be rather muddy, so do go suitably shod.

Distance: 4 ½ miles
OS Map: Explorer 159 Reading
Start: Small free car park at Arborfield Cross, about 200 yards down Swallowfield Rd from The Bull. Grid ref: 760 670

Leaving car park, cross over road turning left along footway towards main road (A327). Use footways to pass anti-clockwise around roundabout and into Sindlesham Road (B3030) opposite. Continue on path then road verge for about ¼ mile. Just before right-hand bend, carefully turn left across road and over stile into field. Keep along edge with hedge on left, then immediately after overhead power lines, fork left over stile into fenced and hedged path to reach gravel area

at entrance to Cloud Stables. If you wish to visit the impressive flint-faced Arborfield parish church of St Bartholomew, built in 1863, turn left along road for some 60 yards.

1 To continue walk turn right along road. Immediately after the Old Reading Room (1881) on left, turn sharp left into winding gravel byway (Cartershill Lane). Soon pass Monk's Cottage and eventually reach gate with farm buildings away to left. Ignore concrete track but turn right through another metal gate and follow similar tree lined track (Barrett's Lane). At overhead power lines keep right, continue down winding track to cross Barkham Brook by footbridge beside ford.

2 At top of short sharp rise, after former farm buildings, turn right along metalled road for some 65 yards, then fork right into wide byway, leading to road (B3030). Here cross over and enter gently climbing tree-lined byway (Gravelpithill Lane). After slight right bend before top of hill, turn left into trees. Emerging from woodland, cross track to follow grass path ahead, with

Carter's Hill from Barrett's Lane

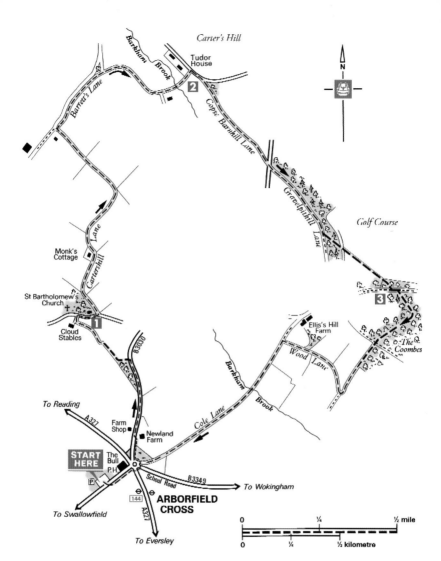

golf course fence on left. From here look left through trees for red-brick Bearwood College.

3 Just beyond corner of golf course, bear left along hard track for some 35 yards, then bear right to reach sandy track (Coombes Lane). Here turn left for about 10 yards, then right, through stileway into path flanked by rhododendrons. Follow this wide path round right-hand bend and continue gently downhill eventually to reach path junction. Here go straight on until, at end of field now on right, turn sharp right into tree-lined path (Wood Lane). At top of climb turn left along slowly descending track (Cole Lane). After crossing Barkham Brook again, by concrete footbridge next to ford, continue on track to eventually reach Arborfield Cross again. Here with care cross road junction into Swallowfield Road to return to car park at start.

DATE WALKED		

Barkham Church and The Coombes

This circular walk, almost entirely in the parish of Barkham, is across pleasant undulating farmland and through a delightful area of woodland just to the south-west of Wokingham.

Distance: 4 miles
OS Map: Explorer 159 Reading
Start: East end of Coombes Lane, at junction with Bearwood Road. Grid ref: 783 678

From the end of Coombes Lane, cross Bearwood Road and continue along Sandy Lane. Beyond the houses it continues as a sunken wooded path. (As an alternative to continuing along the lane walkers may go diagonally across the public open space (Elizabeth Park) presently on the right and find their way through the trees opposite to rejoin it. See map) After three white houses on right, the roadway bears right to reach estate roads just before crossroads ahead (B3349). Here turn right and about half way down Doles Hill, immediately after property 354, turn left into hard track. Where this turns left, go straight on over stile, with fence on left. At road ahead, cross over into path opposite, between fence on left and buildings on right.

1 After stile ahead, bear slightly right down middle of field to stile in far boundary. Here cross track (Nashgrove Ride) and then after stile next to metal gate keep straight on through middle of field ahead. Beyond further stile, continue along field edge beside hedge on left, towards spire of Barkham Church. At end of field cross stiles into churchyard and pass on right St James's Church. Continue ahead along lane past pond (on left) to road junction.

2 Cross road and turn right along footway, then immediately before a white cottage on left, turn left into fenced and hedged path, and over stile. The path runs the length of this long narrow field. After stile beside old metal gate continue, now with hedgerow on left at first. Path goes straight ahead, to right of some trees, then beside hedge again on left, until just beyond isolated red-brick cottage it crosses stile into fenced gravel drive.

3 At Barkham Road (B3349) ahead, with care cross over and turn right along footway for a distance. Then some 70 yards after crossing bridge over Barkham Brook, turn left up broad gravel track. Keep to right of gateway of Rectory and continue keeping slightly right, on climbing woodland path into the Coombes.

4 At path junction turn left through stileway on woodland path, shortly to cross a deep gully via a plank bridge. Beyond the coombe maintain same general direction along winding, waymarked path, soon with bank and ditch nearby on right. Beyond large tree path continues, now with bank on left, to reach footbridge at path junction. Go ahead into narrower path and at end of field on left (Don't be fooled, the small wooden huts in this field are not for chickens – they are for scouts!), pass stileway and climb steep hillside to path junction at top.

5 Here turn right along broad track (Coombes Lane) – shortly on left glimpse across golf course, distant red-brick Bearwood College. On reaching near corner of field on right keep straight on along Coombes Lane to return to start.

DATE WALKED		

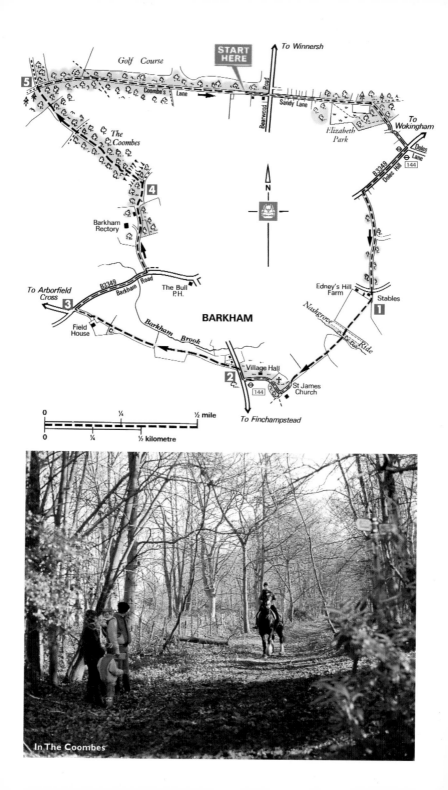

In The Coombes

Burghfield Lock and Calcot Mill

This circular walk, while just on the fringe of urban Reading, meanders through beautiful meadows bordering the Holy Brook and the River Kennet, visiting the century-old Calcot Mill.

Distance: 4 ½ miles
OS Map: Explorer 159 Reading
Start: Car park off Brunel Road, Southcote, signposted 'Southcote Linear Park'. Grid ref: 686 715

With your back to the grass play area join the well-used path outside the car park fence, with the Holy Brook shortly on right. Follow this narrow path, next to stream at first, then beside railway embankment. On reaching a crossing track, turn right under railway arch, then immediately left, along grass strip between railway on left and river. Emerging at another crossing, turn right along this unmade road, over a concrete bridge and on between flood meadows.

1 Follow track where it turns right and within 40 yards climb the steps of an iron-railed footbridge (Milkmaids Bridge) spanning the Kennet & Avon Canal by Southcot Lock. Reaching the towpath, turn left for about 40 yards, then turn right over footbridge (main stream of the River Kennet), then right again, along well-used path following the river, until reaching a weir where river rejoins the canal.

2 Here turn left along towpath, opposite moorings. Path narrows to pass beneath Burghfield Bridge, *built in the early 1800s by canal engineer John Rennie, replacing an earlier swing-bridge. The Kennet Navigation was first opened in 1723, linking Reading to Newbury. In 1810 it became part of the 87-mile long Kennet & Avon Canal to Bristol via Bath. The canal flourished until the railways came in the mid 1800s, but by the 1950s was more or less derelict. In 1962 a Trust was formed by*

local enthusiasts to start restoration work. HM the Queen reopened the canal in 1990. Today British Waterways manages the canal with financial help from the Trust and local authorities.

Follow canal bank past the 'Cunning Man' to reach and turn right over footbridge (Swan Bridge), designed for barge horses to cross. Along here are remains of osier beds which provided willows for basket-making. Soon arrive at Burghfield Lock, seemingly far from the madding crowd. It is interesting to try to 'spot the joins' between the Kennet river and the specially made cuts, on one of which this lock stands.

From lock continue along bank. A stile followed by a raised embankment marks the beginning of a stretch of the old river. After a second stile the official right of way hugs the riverbank but through these meadows it may be easier to use other well-defined paths ahead. At end of meadows climb embankment leading up to bridge (Hissey's Bridge), which do <u>not</u> cross. Instead turn right, down through gate and straight on across meadow towards railway left of power-line poles.

3 Carefully cross railway line ahead through metal gates then turn right to follow again bank of the now familiar Holy Brook. Reaching bridge, do not cross, but bear right, across middle of meadow (keeping parallel to railway) to far corner and continue along tree-lined track with ditch, then stream, on left. Turn left over concrete footbridge and go straight across field ahead with fence on left. Approaching buildings, cross concrete bridge, pass Brook Barn and turn right between parts of the former Calcot Mill.

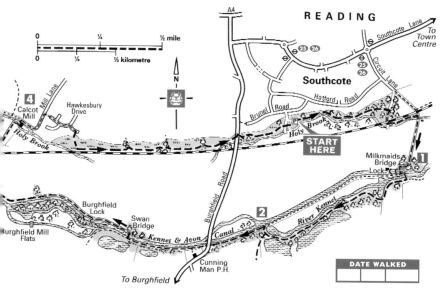

This mill was once part of the Manor of Tilehurst (today in Theale parish) and was held by the monks until Henry VIII dissolved Reading Abbey. Queen Elizabeth I may not have slept here but in 1593 she certainly leased 'a mill at Tilehurst' to her favourite, Robert, Earl of Essex. A working mill until about 1964, it was later largely destroyed by fire. The original stone walls and the still-turning water wheel today form part of the garden alongside the converted Old Granary. Notice also the Coach-house and 18th-century one-time miller's house.

4 From mill follow the shingle drive (a public path) leading onto a road. At top of slope turn right on tarmac path between fences. Continue ahead through bends of estate road (Hawkesbury Drive). At No.41 (on right), bear right for 40 yards, then turn sharp right through swing-gate into grass open space. Bear left across grass on well-used path, soon beside trees on right. This pleasant broad grassland strip leads back in ¾ mile, after crossing Burghfield Road, to car park at start.

The original Swan Bridge – now replaced with a structure more suitable for wheelchair use

Spencers Wood and Priory Farm

This fairly level circular walk covers a variety of scenery – fields, farms and woodland – to the south of the village of Spencers Wood. After wet weather Beech Hill Coverts can be muddy, so do go suitably shod.

Distance: 5 miles
OS Map: Explorer 159 Reading
Start: Basingstoke Rd just south of junction with Hyde End Rd (B3349). Grid ref: 715 666. Buses stop here and cars can be parked on the verge opposite shop and houses.

Cross over Basingstoke Road into Spring Gardens and after some 80 yards keep left into tarmac path, leading to estate road (Larchside Close). Continue ahead until just beyond No. 1 (on right) turn right beside wooden 5-bar gate and follow tree-lined footpath. On reaching roadside (Hyde End Road) turn right along footway for about ¼ mile, to take second turning on right, Sussex Lane, soon becoming a gravel roadway with variety of property. After stile ahead by wooden gate, go on across paddock to another stile.

1 Definitive path now continues ahead for a similar distance, to a waymark post. Here turn right between open fields to reach and bear left along a concrete strip, used for farm storage. Facing an open field, turn left on farm track beside trees to pass farm buildings on right and then, on left, look for moated Sheepbridge Court. Carefully cross road and go straight ahead along wide gravel track beside Mill restaurant. Entering field ahead between posts, turn left along field edge with hedge and trees on left almost hiding the River Loddon. Where field bears right, turn left over plank bridge with stile and along right-hand side of young plantation leading to stile at road.

2 Turn right along lane, then left at T-junction, Lambs Lane. At end of trees on left of lane, turn sharp left down track to pass beneath bypass (A33). On far side turn right up slope and at end of copse turn left over stile. *On left is a copse surrounded by the remains of a moat, known as Beaumys Castle. In 1339 the Lord of the Manor, Nicholas de la Beche (whose family gave its name to the village of Beech Hill), obtained a licence from the King to crenellate (fortify) his house. Perhaps it stood here.*

Footpath follows drive towards The Priory

3 Follow left side of field, cross footbridge and stile in corner, then bear slightly left across field towards conifers and stile into yard of Priory Farm. Continue on same line through concrete yard. *Look on left for well-preserved granary on staddle- stones. Over fence can be seen parts of a very old house, known today as the Priory. In its idyllic Loddon-side setting it was painted in 1821 by John Constable. The earliest building on this site was the 12th-century Hermitage of St Leonard, later converted into a private house. For nearly 500 years until 1924 it belonged to Eton College. It is surely one of Berkshire's most historic houses.*

4 Leaving farmyard, turn right along drive to lodge. Here turn right along roadway (Wood Lane), pass through stileway by gate and continue on bridleway with woodland both sides. Where lane turns right, turn left over

bridleway bridge, then turn left along woodland path. On reaching road (Beech Hill Road) opposite Brook Farm, turn right along grass verge and over bypass. Here cross to left-hand side of road to follow path beside fence. At top of rise bear left along lane giving wide views over countryside. Keep straight on at crossing lane and over stile by rusty gate.

5 Follow woodland path ahead with field close by on right to cross causeway. If path is flooded here retrace your steps and take alternative path on left. (See map) Now turn right for 50 yards along a track (Kiln Lane), turn left over stile and head mid-field towards distant houses on Basingstoke Road and the start.

DATE WALKED		

Hurst Village and River Loddon

This circular walk passes through the largely unspoilt village of Hurst and surrounding meadows, returning along the banks of the River Loddon on a path created in 1991 – a 'planning gain' from nearby gravel extraction.

Distance: Just over 4 miles
OS Map: Explorer 159 Reading
Start: Free car park in Sandford Lane, Hurst, opposite Black Swan Sailing Club.
Grid ref: 787 727

From car park entrance, turn left along the lane past Park Cottage and follow grass verge. Outside the main gates of Hurst Grove turn right and shortly cross carefully into Dunt Lane for a few yards, before turning left over stile. Start by following headland path towards buildings (Hatch Gate Farm) then cut across field corner to reach a stile onto footbridge. Go straight ahead along road for 100 yards before

Footpath to the Green Man

bearing left into short track, to enter field ahead at stile by gate. Take diagonal line towards church tower, then bear left beside fence to road.

1 After second kissing gate turn right up lane. *The original Church of St Nicholas dates from the 12th-century. The tower was built in 1612, the south side and porch being added in 1875. The Almshouses opposite were built in 1682 as a 'Hospital for the maintenance of 8 poor persons at 6d per diem (day) for ever'. (Inflation had not been invented!) Further along stands the Castle Inn, still with a bowling green said to have been laid in 1628 for the benefit of Charles I.*

As an alternative to following the road past the Castle, we can take the gravel path leading behind the church tower. *Here, ignominiously situated near the compost heap you will find a charming and most unusual memorial to the local blacksmith, Thomas Brent.* Behind the church follow path bearing left into graveyard to reach road. Here turn left, with care along the lane.

2 Just beyond Old School House turn right into Orchard Road and at end of field on left, turn left directly across two fields (passing through a pair of gates between them) to reach stile into School Road. Turn right, passing the infants school (built in 1843), crossing to left-hand footway leading to village pond. Cross junction ahead into Hinton Road, continuing on left-hand footway as far as the Green Man.

3 Immediately opposite the pub cross stile to take path through middle of paddock to lane with stiles either side. Now follow field-edge and shortly join lane by Little Farm. Keep left of thatched cottage ahead to enter a 'green lane' (Hogmore Lane). At first field entrance on left cross footbridge/stile, turning right to follow hedge through two fields, leading to main road opposite Broadwater Cottages.

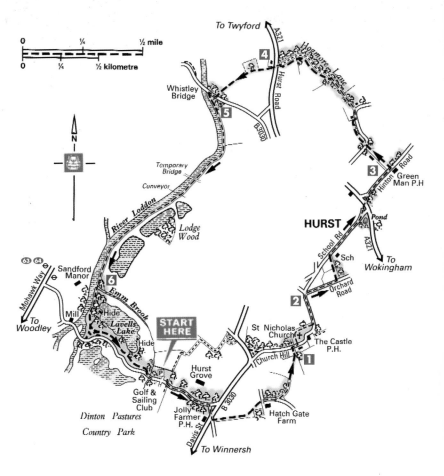

To Twyford

Whistley Bridge

Hurst Road

A321

B3030

Temporary Bridge

Conveyor

River Loddon

Lodge Wood

Sandford Manor

Mohawk Way

63 64

To Woodley

Mill

Hide

Lavells Lake

Hide

Emm Brook

START HERE

Hurst Grove

Golf & Sailing Club

Dinton Pastures Country Park

Jolly Farmer P.H.

Davis St

B3030

To Winnersh

St Nicholas Church

Church Hill

The Castle P.H.

Hatch Gate Farm

Orchard Road

School Rd

HURST

Pond

Hinton Road

Green Man P.H

A321

To Wokingham

Sch

4 Carefully cross busy road (A321) and take broad gravel track left of cottages (upgraded from footpath to bridleway after gravel extraction). Emerging at road, turn right for 45 yards, then left onto gravel track. *At this point, just ahead along the lane stands the pretty Whistley Bridge House – well worth a look. Domesday Book records a mill at Whistley, 'valued at 5 shillings and 250 eels'.*

5 Returning to the gravel path, this very shortly joins grass path beside the River Loddon which we follow for just over a mile. *On the left along here once stood an old manor house, Whistley Court, pulled down in the mid 1800s. Can you find any traces of the inlet from the riverbank which once led to its thatched boat house?*

6 After gravel workings the stream-side path crosses modern footbridge over the Emm Brook. When opposite the (converted) white weather boarded Sandford Mill with its private island, look out for path leading back left towards Teal hide, one of two hides overlooking Lavells Lake – excellent spots for watching wildlife, including foxes!

Just before swing-gate at road ahead, turn back sharp left on broad grass path. Keep on this broad path as it follows the roadside hedge (a firm path bears off left to Tern hide) and eventually leads over a footbridge back to car park at start.

DATE WALKED
26 8 13

Twyford Mill & Charvil Meadows to Borough Bridge

An easy stroll from Twyford passing through a BBONT nature reserve, Charvil Meadows and visiting two Thames backwaters with views towards Shiplake.

Distance: 4 miles
OS Map: Explorer 159 Reading
Start: Polehampton Close car park in Twyford.

Unfortunately, following a public inquiry in 2007, a government inspector chose not to confirm an order recognising the one-mile section of Loddon Drive from Borough Bridge to Wargrave Station that we had previously incorporated into this guidebook, as a presumed public right of way.

Over 130 walkers, mostly Wargrave & Charvil residents, submitted evidence to the local inquiry showing pedestrian use – in some cases for more than 60 years, without being challenged or passing signs bringing into question their right to walk along it. Despite this weight of evidence, and the publication of four previous editions of this guidebook we are now obliged to terminate our route description on the attractive Borough Bridge where the definitive path stops at the parish boundary.*

Walkers who would like to see the remaining 'lost' half of Loddon Drive added to the definitive map, should write to Wokingham Borough Council and ask for a Path Creation Order to be made. Without this missing link Wargrave is virtually cut off from its riverside neighbours and from any easy access to the Thames Path National Trail. Responsible walkers have used the path for many years; it would be a tragedy if this could not continue.

From car park, pass library on right and at top of slope opposite Twyford's oldest building (an Elizabethan farmhouse), turn left into High Street.

Borough Bridge

1 Go over railway and opposite 18th-century Mill House, turn left on public footpath across the former mill stream (A mill stood here from 1363 until 1998). After two footbridges close together, path follows right bank of stream to mill pool, crosses bridge over main stream of River Loddon and turns left to follow the bank. With railway viaduct shortly ahead, path turns away from river and keeps left, soon with embankment on left and lake on right. Look for gap on left where path leads under rail arch then follow route ahead leading to minor road.

2 Here turn right for twenty yards, then bear left into footpath, crossing footbridge. Go slightly left across meadow to white rails on far side (Giddy Bridge). Continue on path to left of Lands End pub, turning right across forecourt, then right again for 20 yards down lane. Here turn left through swing-gate into Charvil Country Park.

From gate turn right along perimeter grass path as it circles to left, soon between lake on left and river on right (Loddon Old River). After another gate go under rail arch, then head slightly right for some 60 yards to cross wooden footbridge. Keep alongside trees ahead until, just before they finish,